# Sports Illustrated
# BADMINTON

*The Sports Illustrated Library*

BOOKS ON TEAM SPORTS

| Baseball | Curling: Techniques and Strategy | Ice Hockey |
| Basketball | Football: Defense | Soccer |
| | Football: Offense | Volleyball |

BOOKS ON INDIVIDUAL SPORTS

| Badminton | Horseback Riding | Table Tennis |
| Fly Fishing | Skiing | Tennis |
| Golf | Squash | Track and Field: Running Events |

BOOKS ON WATER SPORTS

| Powerboating | Small Boat Sailing |
| Skin Diving and Snorkeling | Swimming and Diving |

SPECIAL BOOKS

| Dog Training | Training with Weights |
| Safe Driving | |

# Sports Illustrated
# BADMINTON

By J. FRANK DEVLIN
with REX LARDNER
and the Editors of
Sports Illustrated

Illustrations by
George Janes

J. B. LIPPINCOTT COMPANY
Philadelphia and New York

U. S. Library of Congress Cataloging in Publication Data

Devlin, J   Frank.
    Sports illustrated badminton.

    (The Sports illustrated library)
    First ed., by the editors of Sports illustrated, published
under title: Book of badminton.
        1. Badminton (Game) I. Sports illustrated (Chicago)
II. Sports illustrated (Chicago) Book of badminton. III. Title.
GV1007.D42 1973        796.34'5        72–10556
ISBN–0–397–00967–4
ISBN–0–397–00968–2 (pbk.)

Cover photograph: Don Bender

Photographs on pages 8 and 20: American Badminton Association

Photograph on page 52: J. Frank Devlin

Photographs on pages 76 and 82: United Press International

Photograph on page 79: John H. Hessey, IV

Printed in the United States of America

Revised 1973, Third Printing

# Contents

# Sports Illustrated
# BADMINTON

# 1
# The Game

THE GAME of badminton is deceptive. Few sports are as much fun to engage in from the moment you step onto the court. The racket is light and easily managed, and the bird, or shuttlecock, is not difficult to hit over the net. If you miss, the bird can be quickly recovered and a rally is started anew. After the basics of timing, footwork and stroking are learned, rallies are long and you can enjoy a good deal of pleasant, healthful exercise.

As you gain in experience, however, you will find that badminton requires subtleties and skills that make it different from all other racket games, and in some respects more difficult. The court is relatively small—which means that in singles you do not have a large area to cover, but also means that to place a shot out of your opponent's reach and still keep it within bounds you must hit with fine precision. Badminton, like baseball, is a game of inches. A characteristic of the game is that you must strike the bird before it hits the surface of the court. This means, in many cases, that you must actively pursue the bird and must, under pressure, be able to hit a return that will not allow your opponent to work you out of position.

The game can be played both indoors and out, although in the outdoor version the bird, because of its lightness, is apt to be wafted off course by the slightest breeze. The outdoor game, therefore, is one of less precision, but under favorable conditions it is every bit as exciting and demanding as the game played indoors. Many fine players have developed their skill while playing outdoors, and in some Asian countries, where there are now many indoor as well as outdoor courts, the game is very nearly the national sport. The Malaysians, Indonesians and Japanese, because of their enthusiasm for badminton and their agility and endurance, are among the world's best players. A person's dexterity and stamina, combined with a good sense of tactics, are much more important than his size and power.

Due to the extreme lightness of the bird and its tendency to lose speed rapidly after being hit, proper stroking is essential to make use of the extreme boundaries of the court. A player whose shot production is faulty and who therefore burns up extra energy in hitting his strokes is likely to lose to a more experienced opponent. The lightness of the tools of the game adds another element: the direction the bird takes can be determined by an almost imperceptible turn of the wrist made at the last split second before striking. Thus, deception becomes a valuable ally in making things difficult for your opponent.

One of the main distinctions between badminton and all other racket games is the length of the rallies. The bird can cross the net twenty-five or thirty times before a point is finally won. Good players seldom miss any but an extremely difficult shot. Patience, therefore, is a necessary quality for the truly ambitious badminton player to develop. So is excellent physical condition.

Badminton, in short, is fun to play when you first pick up a racket, and as you grow more proficient it becomes a game of great challenge. The pleasure you will find in badminton—a fine social game, a splendid conditioner and one of the most popular of carry-over sports—will increase as you acquire a sound knowledge of tactics and of team play in doubles, the ability to outfox your opponents and the knack of placing the bird exactly where you wish.

# 2
# Clothing
# and Equipment

THE CLOTHING you wear for playing badminton indoors should be loose and comfortable. The preferred color is white. A man usually wears shorts and a T shirt or sweat-shirt, and a woman tennis skirt or shorts and a tennis blouse. Clothing should be of a type that does not retain moisture readily. A light wool sweater is useful when warming up.

In the outdoor game, which is usually more informal, almost any clothing can be worn—though tennis clothing is advised—with emphasis on practicality. Since so many shots are taken overhead, it may be helpful to wear a hat or cap with a visor.

Shoes should fit securely and, for the indoor game, provide good cushioning against a hard floor. A tennis shoe with a rubber sole is recommended for indoor play, a tennis shoe with a ridged sole for outdoor play. For extra protection of the feet, it is sometimes helpful to wear two pairs of wool socks.

In selecting a racket, you have a choice of light, medium

or heavy. From 4½ to 5 ounces is the average weight. You should choose the weight that feels most comfortable—one that allows you to swing with a minimum of effort and muscular strain. Ideally, the racket, as you swing it, should feel like an extension of your arm.

The handle should fit comfortably in the hand, but it is better to get a grip that is too large rather than one too small. An undersized grip is likely to reduce the amount of wrist action you can utilize. The handle should be octagonal in shape, not round or oval, and the broader facets should be parallel to the face of the racket. The shape of the handle is an aid to the player in determining, without looking, whether he has the right grip or not.

A racket strung with gut costs $20 to $30; one strung with nylon will cost about $3 less. (Gut is considered to be better than nylon, although nylon may last longer and is advised for beginners.) The racket should be kept in a press when not in use and protected from moisture.

Birds are of two main types—feathered, with a cork base, and plastic. They weigh from 73 to 85 grains, with the average weight about 76 grains. Plastic birds with rubberized bases are fine for outdoor play (they are slightly heavier than feathered birds), but the feathered variety is better for indoor play. Beginners, however, may prefer to start with plastic birds, since their lifetime is considerably longer than that of feathered birds. While no special care is necessary for plastic birds, feathered ones should be kept in a cool, damp place when not in use. The price of plastic birds is about $3 for six, while that of feathered birds is about $2 for three. The price of birds and rackets varies widely from store to store, from season to season, and also with the quantities purchased.

# 3
# Basic Rules
# and Scoring

TO DEVELOP stroke proficiency quickly and to understand the rules and basic tactics of the game, the beginner should start with singles.

The complete laws of badminton are set down at the back of this book, but here are some fundamental rules and the method of keeping score:

(1) Play at the start of a game begins with the serve being delivered from the right half court to a receiver standing in *his* right half court. (The serve is always made diagonally.)

(2) Only the server can score points. In singles, if the server loses a rally, he relinquishes the serve and becomes the receiver. (The rules of serving in doubles are discussed later.) After the server wins a point, he moves to the left half court and serves diagonally to his opponent's left half court. In most cases, the player who first scores 15 points in men's singles, or 11 points in women's singles,

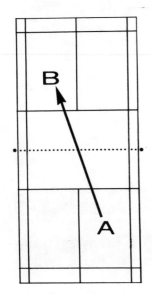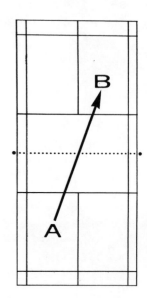

In singles, server A always serves diagonally to receiver B. After winning a point, A serves from the left court and B receives in his left court.

wins the game. There are, however, a few exceptions to this rule. In men's singles and in all doubles games, when the score is tied at 13-all, the player who first reached the 13th point has the option of "setting" the game at 5 or refusing to set it. The winner is the player who first wins the number of points that have been set; or, if there is no set, the first to reach 15. If he decides to set, the score is called "love-all" and the side which first scores 5 points wins the game. However, if the player decides not to set then, if the score should become 14-all the side which first reached 14 has the option of setting the game to 3, and the side which first scores 3 points wins the game.

(3) In the case of a 9-all tie in ladies' singles, the player who first reached 9 has the option of setting the game at 3 points. If the option is refused, the winner is the first player to reach 11. If the score is tied at 10-all, the player who first reached 10 has the option of setting the game

at 2 points. If the option is refused, the winner is the player who first reaches 11 points.

(4) Two out of three games generally decides a match in both men's and women's play.

(5) It is customary for players to change courts at the end of each game, and the winner serves first in the following game. In a match, to ensure even conditions, players change sides in the third game when the leading score, in men's play, reaches 8. In women's play, the change of sides occurs when the leading score reaches 6.

(6) During a game, when the server's score consists of an even number—2, 4, 6, etc.—he always serves from his right half court. (The opponent's score is considered only when he is serving.)

(7) The server, as a consequence, changes from his right half court to his left and back again after each point he wins; but if he loses a rally and relinquishes the serve in a particular court, the next time he serves it is from that same court. To avoid confusion, the score should be clearly announced by one player or the other immediately after the serve changes hands. The server's score is announced first.

## SOME BASIC RULES OF PLAY

(1) Both the server and receiver must stand within the boundaries of their respective half courts until the server strikes the bird. Touching the boundary lines of these courts before the server strikes the bird is a foul. In an officiated match, the server would lose the serve if he committed this foul; the receiver, if he committed it, would lose the point.

(2) The server is allowed only one serve.

(3) Shots that hit the lines are considered good.

(4) A serve that hits the net and falls over into the

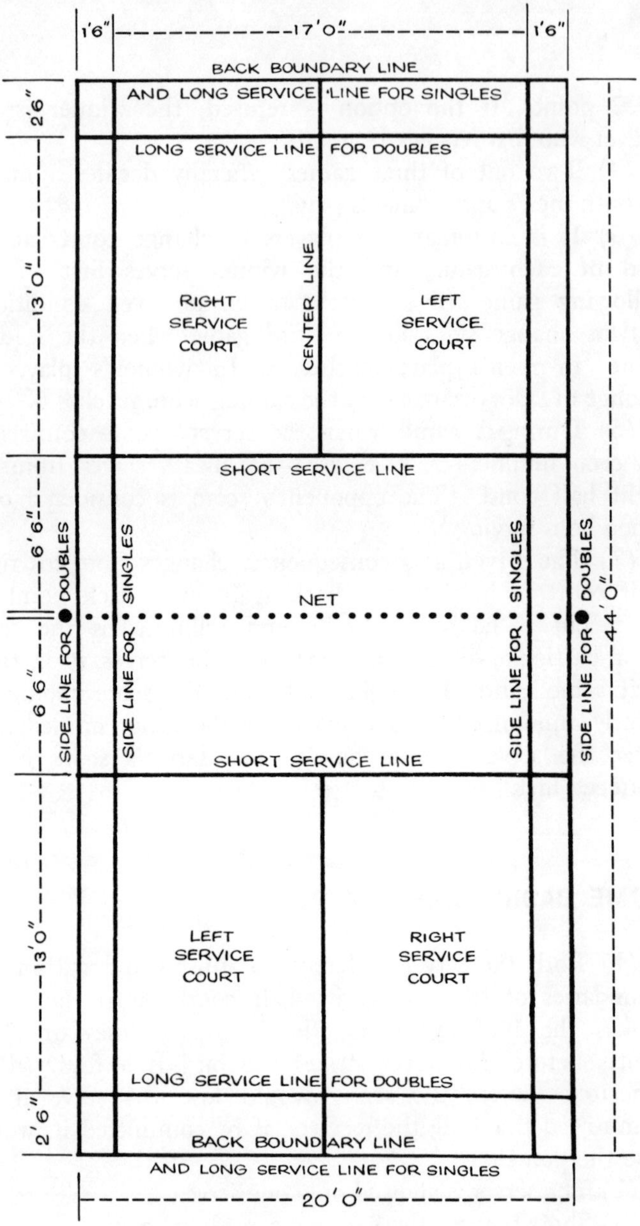
1'6"
17'0"
1'6"
BACK BOUNDARY LINE
AND LONG SERVICE LINE FOR SINGLES
2'6"
LONG SERVICE LINE FOR DOUBLES
13'0"
RIGHT SERVICE COURT
CENTER LINE
LEFT SERVICE COURT
SHORT SERVICE LINE
6'6"
SIDE LINE FOR DOUBLES
SIDE LINE FOR SINGLES
NET
SIDE LINE FOR SINGLES
SIDE LINE FOR DOUBLES
44'0"
6'6"
SHORT SERVICE LINE
13'0"
LEFT SERVICE COURT
RIGHT SERVICE COURT
LONG SERVICE LINE FOR DOUBLES
2'6"
BACK BOUNDARY LINE
AND LONG SERVICE LINE FOR SINGLES
20'0"

The court

opponent's court is a good serve and should be played; one that hits the net and does not fall into the proper court is at fault and the receiver thereupon becomes the server.

(5) If the server misses the bird completely while serving and it does not touch any part of his body or clothing before falling to the surface of the court, he may serve over.

(6) Should a player miss the bird completely in attempting a return and it fall out of bounds, he wins the point if he is the server, or takes the serve, but doesn't win the point if he is the receiver.

(7) During a rally, if a player hits the net with his racket, body or clothing, he is considered to have lost the rally. The racket may be swung over the net after the bird is struck, but it is a foul if the bird is struck on the opponent's side of the net.

(8) It is now considered legal to hit the bird on the wooden part of the racket. If the return goes over the net and into the opponent's court, it must be played.

## COURT, BASIC RULES AND SCORING IN DOUBLES

(1) In doubles, each service court is 2 feet 6 inches shorter than in singles, but 1 foot 6 inches wider. The back boundary line is the same for both games after the bird is in play, but each sideline in doubles extends 1 foot 6 inches beyond the singles sidelines.

(2) As in singles, a flip of a coin or the spin of a racket determines who serves first. In the first inning (an inning is the turn of one side to serve), only the partner in the right half court serves. After that, players on a particular side alternate the serve in each inning for the rest of the game.

(3) After the first serve, service alternates from one court to the other. The receivers do not alternate courts

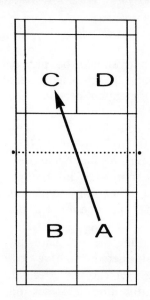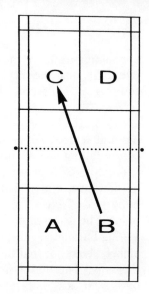

In doubles the server always starts from the right court. Server and his partner alternate courts as points are won but the receiving team does not change courts.

while they are the receiving side. When the first server in an inning loses the serve, his partner serves from the alternate half court—not from the court his partner last served from.

(4) The first serve in every inning is always from the right-hand half court (as opposed to singles, where it may be made from either half court, depending on the score). The same server does not necessarily always serve from this court, however, because every time a point is won the serving side alternates courts, and when the side loses the serve the partners remain where they are to receive. When they regain the serve, the partner who happens to be in the right half court serves first.

A typical pair of innings might go like this: Server A (with partner B) serves from the right half court to receiver C. A's side wins the point, so A moves to the left half court and B moves to the right half court, while C and partner D stay where they are.

A loses the serve from the left half court, putting his side out, since, in the first inning, a side has only one serve. C, being in his side's right half court, now serves to B, who is in *his* side's right half court. C loses his serve, so D now serves from the left half court to A. D's side winning the point, C moves to the right half court and serves to B. D loses the serve and B, being in the right half court, thereupon serves first for his side. D becomes the receiver in his side's right half court, while C will receive in the left half court.

(5) During service, the partner of the server and the partner of the receiver may stand in any part of the court so long as they do not interfere with the serve.

(6) As a check on the score in doubles, when a player serves or receives in the court he was in at the start of the game, his side's score should be an even number of points (or zero). If he is not in his original service or receiving court, his side's score should be an odd number of points.

(7) As in singles, the score should be announced every time the serve changes sides, with the score of the serving team given first.

(8) In the first inning of a mixed doubles match, the woman usually serves first. This is not necessarily a matter of courtesy—it allows the woman to move forward toward the net after serving and the man to cover the back of the court so that both players can perform to their best advantage.

(9) A game in both men's and women's doubles and in mixed doubles consists of 15 points. The rules for "setting the game at scores of 13-all and 14-all are the same as in singles, with one member of the side that reaches 13 or 14 first being allowed the option of setting the game or announcing "No set"—in which case, the winning team is the one that first reaches 15.

# 4
# The Grips

AS IN any racket game, holding the racket correctly is of prime importance. Ideally, the grip in badminton should permit easy and supple movement of the wrist, allowing the wrist to impart snap and power when desired and to apply delicacy of touch when that is called for. A turn of the wrist, made at the split second before you strike the bird, can likewise change the direction of the shot, adding deception to your strokes.

Every beginner should pay attention to acquiring the right grip for both the forehand and the backhand before making the first shots. Bad habits acquired when the racket is first grasped and the initial strokes are made are difficult to overcome. It is unfortunate that some of today's good players hold their rackets incorrectly; they have attained high rank in spite of the grips they use.

The word "grip" is used here, but a more accurate term might be "hold." In badminton, it is essential not to grip the racket tightly. To do so is to decrease the suppleness of the wrist. The bird is extremely light and so is the racket; you do not need the locked wrist and tight grip used in tennis. The racket should be held firmly, but if your grip is one of iron, neither delicate nor forceful shots can be played.

## THE FOREHAND GRIP

For the forehand—as in tennis—the basic instruction is "shake hands with the racket." This permits easy movement of the wrist and gives the fingers good control over the racket handle. Here are the specific steps to take in assuming the forehand grip:

(1) Hold the racket by the shaft in your left hand, with the frame perpendicular to the floor.

(2) With your right hand, shake hands with the handle. The right forefinger should be slightly spread from the other fingers for better control. The heel of the hand should be pressed against the leather base.

(3) As a check, drop the head of the racket by lowering the elbow. If the racket lies flat along the calf of your right leg, you are holding the racket correctly for the forehand.

## THE BACKHAND GRIP

The backhand grip is assumed by giving the racket a half-turn to the right and moving the thumb along the back of the handle. This gives good support to the racket for shots on the backhand side and allows free play of the wrist. The advantage of this thumb-up grip is the benefit you gain from the thrust of the thumb in all backhand strokes.

While some players believe that there is not time to change grips during a rally, experience shows that with practice it can be done quite easily. In changing from forehand to backhand or vice versa, the left hand is not used; you merely loosen your hold on the racket, turn it slightly and assume the new hold.

22

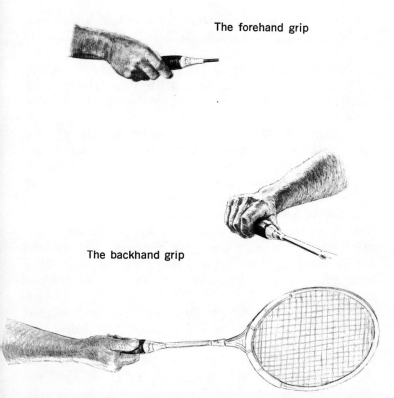

The forehand grip

The backhand grip

The backhand grip, showing control of the racket by the thumb

## THE FLAT GRIP

A third type of grip, used in special cases, is the "flat grip." For this, the palm and the heel of the hand are utilized for support more than the fingers, and the grip can be likened to the old "Western grip" in tennis. This grip is used almost exclusively in doubles—in two different situations: when you plan to rush a low serve and when you are positioned close to the net during a rally, looking for a feeble shot that you can poke down steeply for the point.

23

When this grip is used, the racket is held almost vertically, with the frame a little bit higher than the head. It is assumed that if the opportunity arises to make the shot the bird will be coming toward you so fast that there will be time to make only the briefest backswing and no time to change from a forehand to a backhand grip or vice versa.

To assume the flat grip, lay the racket on a table, place your fingers on the handle, pick it up and hold it vertically in front of your face. The V formed by the thumb and forefinger should point toward the floor when the face of the racket is parallel to the net.

It can be seen that this grip is of little use for lifting low shots, but it does allow the racket with very little preparation to be in position for shots either at net-tape height or a foot or so higher. The racket is already *there*. Your partner can retrieve shots that are too high for you to reach.

While this grip is far less important than the backhand and forehand grips, it should be practiced by ladies who play a lot of mixed doubles (since close to the net usually is the position they play best) and also by men who play men's doubles or mixed. In replying to a low serve, the male player can rush toward it and hit it without a split second's delay because the racket face is already parallel to the net and no backswing is necessary.

Consistently attacking in this manner with the flat grip can put a great deal of pressure on the server in doubles, where the low serve is principally relied on. If, of course, your opponent hits a high serve, you can quickly change your grip to the most suitable one as you move back in the court to get under the bird.

# 5
# Serves

THE SERVE in badminton—unlike that in all other racket games—is essentially a defensive shot, a means of putting the bird in play. Because of the rules that state (1) that the serve is a fault if the bird is struck higher than the waist and (2) that the racket hand cannot be brought up higher than the waist, the server is forced to hit upward over a hazard to a waiting opponent. A poor serve can be smashed by an alert receiver who, if he does not win the point outright, has at least put the receiver in a defensive position. Inasmuch as deception is one of the best weapons the server has, he should practice delivering the various types of serves with similar motions.

The serves you should practice most are the *high serve* (used mainly in singles) and the *low*, or *short, serve* (used mainly in doubles). The two other serves are the *flick* and the *drive*. Many Asiatic players use a backhand serve—hit in front of the server's body and struck with pronounced wrist speed.

The reason why the high serve is more popular in singles and the low serve more popular in doubles is that in singles the court into which the serve must be hit is

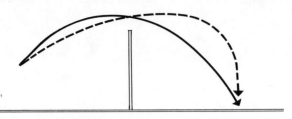

Comparison of an effective low serve (solid line) with an ineffective one (dotted line). Trajectory of the latter makes it susceptible to a hard, steeply hit return.

30 inches longer than it is in doubles, although it is 18 inches narrower.

## THE HIGH SERVE

To deliver the high serve in your opponent's right-hand court, stand in your right half court, close to the middle line and about 4 feet behind the front service line. It is a mistake to stand too close to the net, as then your low serve—should you use that—will have to rise sharply to pass over it. Therefore, you run the risk of letting the bird remain higher than the net tape for a longer period of time than if its trajectory were flatter. This, of course, makes it more vulnerable to attack.

Your left foot should be advanced and your left shoulder should be turned somewhat toward the net. Weight is on the right foot. Hold the bird by the base, between the thumb and forefinger—not by the feathers. The arm is swung back and the wrist is fully cocked, placing the head of the racket behind the right leg.

Toss the bird a few inches into the air, bring the racket smoothly forward as weight is transferred from the right

Holding the bird for the serve

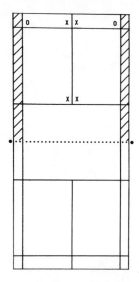

Most effective aim points
for serve in singles:
X—best; O—next best.

foot to the left and, at the split second before striking, bring the wrist sharply upward, imparting extra impetus to the stroke. After the bird is hit, the racket should move in a smooth follow-through in the direction of the bird's flight.

Ideally, the high serve should soar over your opponent's head and then fall perpendicularly to within a few inches of the back service line. The most effective and safe serve from the right-hand court is one that travels to the receiver's backhand side. As you gain in experience, you will find it advantageous to vary your serves according to the weaknesses of your opponent and the positions he takes to receive.

In serving to the left-hand court—that is, the court to the receiver's left—your left foot is again advanced and your left shoulder is turned even more toward the net. The stroke is made like the serve to the first court, with the wrist leading the racket all the way through the shot until the split second before you hit the bird. The most effective place to deliver the high serve in this court is deep to your opponent's forehand. While you are present-

27

1

2

The serve

3

ing him with a forehand smash, you are not allowing him a wide angle in which to hit his return. This makes whatever stroke he plays easier to cover.

## THE LOW SERVE

The low serve is hit with the same preparation as the high serve, but the bird is "persuaded" over the net rather than hit. The arm makes the same backswing and forward motion, but wrist action, before the bird is struck, is more deliberate. The purpose of the serve is to direct the bird's trajectory as close to the net as possible while hitting it hard enough to keep it from falling in front of your opponent's service court.

The best place to direct a low serve from your right half court is to the backhand of a right-handed opponent; from your left half court, to the forehand of a right-

28

4                                                  5                    6

handed opponent. By keeping the service in the approxi-mate middle of the playing court, you limit the amount of angle available for your opponent's reply. Of course, if you find a definite backhand weakness, you should take advantage of it by directing repeated low serves there.

If your low serves are being attacked by the receiver because they are coming in too high, edge over slightly to the right in your right-hand half court and to the left in the left-hand half court. Hitting cross-court in this man-ner will tend to flatten out the parabola of the bird, allowing it merely to skim the net and fall quickly. If you do move over, you must be prepared to defend the open spot in your court, however, since the receiver's reply probably will be directed there.

Short serves should be mixed with high ones in both singles and doubles so that your opponent will not be able to anticipate where the bird will come.

## THE FLICK SERVE

The flick serve is a serve somewhere between the short serve and the high one. It is hit with a certain amount of wrist snap but does not have the high trajectory of the conventional high serve. It is useful mainly when your opponent is standing well up in the court, prepared to rush a low serve. The flick should pass over his head, but it should not be so high that he has time to rush back and make a proper stroke. If he hits the return from an off-balance position, he may send you a shot that can easily be put away.

## THE DRIVE SERVE

The drive serve is a low, driven shot usually directed to your opponent's backhand from the right court, and to his forehand from the left court. Stand near the outer border of either court to deliver it. Hit hard with a low trajectory, using a motion that leans toward sidearm. (The toss of the bird for this serve causes it to fall a little farther away from the body than usual.)

Another aim point for the drive serve is directly at your opponent's chest. The purpose of this tactic is to force him to make a cramped stroke. If not used too often, the drive serve is usually good for a quick point.

# 6
# Clears

THIS STROKE, analogous to the deep lob in tennis, is
the one used most frequently in badminton. Like the tennis lob, it can be offensive (when it is hit over the head
of an opponent who is close to the net, making him
scramble back to the baseline) or defensive (when time
must be gained to get back into position or when it is
the safest stroke to make during a rally). In doubles, it
is frequently used to enable your partner to get back into
position.

The clear can be hit either overhand or underhand, on
the backhand and the forehand. It looks like an easy shot
to make, but against a good player it must be hit deep
and high or it will be severely smashed or delicately
dropped over the net. Either reply to the clear demands
an underhand return if it does not win the point outright.
You should develop the ability to hit a clear within a foot
of the baseline from any position in the court, on both
forehand and backhand.

1

Overhead clear                    2

In most cases, the clear requires a good deal of power, making footwork extremely important. This ensures that the body does its full share of the work, assisting the wrist, arm and shoulder in hitting the stroke. Often the first sign of serious fatigue in a game is when a player's clears no longer reach the back of his opponent's court.

## THE OVERHEAD CLEAR—FOREHAND

For several reasons it is sounder to clear overhead than underhand. If you can get to the bird on time, this is the stroke you should use. When you bring your racket back for an overhead clear, your opponent does not generally know if you are going to clear, hit an overhead drop or smash. Also, on some shots, by moving in you can hit the bird a split second sooner, which may put your opponent at a disadvantage. And finally, many players find this shot easier to control than the underhand shot, since it approximates the action of throwing overhand, a familiar motion to most Americans.

32

3

4

For the overhead stroke on the forehand, the feet are placed as they are for the underhand stroke—left foot advanced, weight on the right foot. The body is at about a right angle to the net and the racket is brought back as though for a smash. That is, the elbow is sharply bent, the right hand is close to the right ear and the racket lies almost horizontal behind the head, with the racket face close to the left shoulder blade. The wrist is cocked.

The racket is brought forward in a kind of throwing motion, the wrist remaining cocked. Weight is transferred from the rear to the front foot, the elbow straightens and just before the bird is hit, at a point slightly behind the right shoulder, the wrist is uncocked, lending power to the stroke. You should follow through along the line of flight

33

of the bird, bringing the racket down smoothly. At the
conclusion of the stroke, the racket is at about waist height
on the left side of the body.

## THE OVERHEAD CLEAR—BACKHAND

For many players, this is the most difficult stroke in
badminton—and it is the one your opponent would generally most like to force you to make. As far as deception
is concerned, you can vary the backhand clear with only
one other stroke—the backhand overhead drop. (When
taken in the forecourt and hit very quickly, this shot is
often referred to as a backhand "smash.")

As you move into position to make the stroke, you
quickly change to the backhand grip. The body turns so
that the back is nearly to the net, the right foot is placed
several feet closer to the left sideline than the left foot,
the body is bent slightly away from the net and weight
is placed on the left foot. While these movements are
being made, the racket is brought back. The elbow is
high, pointing toward the bird, and the wrist is cocked.

When the bird is approximately over the right shoulder,
the arm uncoils, weight is transferred to the right foot,
the hand, shoulder and arm bring the racket forward, and,
just before impact, the wrist snaps forward. Racket-head
speed is controlled largely by the thumb as the bird is
struck. The follow-through moves along the line of the
shot. At its conclusion, the arm should be outstretched.

If you are not getting enough distance with your clears,
even though your footwork and your arm and shoulder
motion are correct, you are probably not getting ready
early enough in your swing.

On the other hand, if your clears are going out, you
are probably hitting the bird too late in your swing. To
correct this, meet the bird solidly as you bring your arm
around and concentrate on giving it plenty of loft. If it

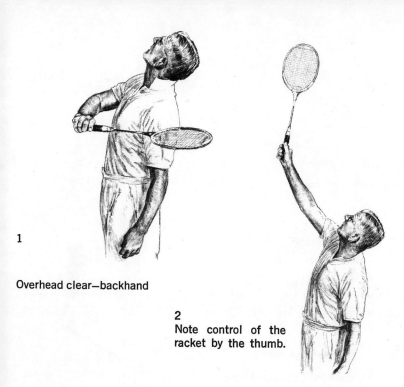

1

Overhead clear—backhand

2
**Note control of the racket by the thumb.**

goes higher, the distance in length it travels will decrease somewhat.

## THE UNDERHAND CLEAR—FOREHAND

Start this stroke with the racket held well back—about on a level with the right shoulder. Your body should be at nearly a right angle to the net, with the left foot about 18 inches forward of the right. At the beginning of the swing, the weight should be on the rear foot. The swing is downward and to the side, with the wrist leading the racket throughout—up to the point just before the bird is struck. During the forward swing, the weight is transferred to the left foot. The more pronounced the wrist action, the better. The follow-through brings the racket

*35*

1

2

Underhand clear—backhand

relatively high—the right hand stopping at about chest height. The elbow is bent and the arm points in the approximate direction of the aim point of the shot.

## THE UNDERHAND CLEAR—BACKHAND

After a bit of practice, most players find it easier to clear on the backhand side than the forehand—the reason being that, in turning their right shoulder far around to make the stroke properly, they automatically move their body out of the way.

As you move into position to make the stroke, quickly shift to the backhand grip and draw the racket far back. The right elbow is sharply bent and the right hand is a

36

3

4

little below and in front of the left biceps. Weight is placed on the left, or rear, foot. As the stroke is made, the right foot should be about 2 feet closer to the left sideline than the left foot and the right knee is slightly bent. This ensures the powerful coiling and uncoiling action necessary for hitting a powerful underhand clear on the backhand. The closer to the surface of the court the shot is taken, the more pronounced the bend of the knee.

Watching the bird carefully, bring the racket forward as your body rapidly turns to the right. Weight is transferred to the forward foot, and the racket (its head speed controlled mainly by the thumb) is snapped forward and up by the hand and wrist. The follow-through brings the racket relatively high. At the end of the stroke the arm is straight and the hand is at about head level.

Preparing to hit an underhand clear
from a position close to the floor

Follow-through of
low backhand clear

If underhand clears are falling short even though foot-work and wrist action are correct, it is probably because you are hitting them too late. To achieve proper length, get into position sooner and hit earlier.

If your underhand clears are getting too much length and not enough height, hit more positively and concentrate on giving the shot more loft.

# 7
# The Smash

THE SMASH is a tempting shot. You are on the attack, and if you hit it properly you may win the point. It is pleasant to be so aggressive and force your opponent to scramble for the return.

But for many players—despite their instinct to hit down and hit hard—the smash is a dangerous shot. They use the smash too frequently, without the desired effect and at the sacrifice of a great deal of energy. Beginning players, overestimating the value of this stroke as a point winner, smash at every opportunity—often when their opponent can, without much difficulty, make a return that will keep the rally going or even put the smasher in trouble.

Badminton, as has been noted, is a game of condition. A player who smashes consistently is very likely to tire as the game continues, and his shots will become less accurate and less forceful. Against an alert, experienced opponent he will find his attacking play less effective and he will soon be on the defensive. Seeing one's smashes come back time after time is also very discouraging psychologically and cannot help but reduce a player's confidence.

On the other hand, an energetic player without a great deal of experience or tactical knowledge may find the smash, if used judiciously, his most powerful weapon. Not only will it win points but it may cause his opponent to make errors in an effort to neutralize it. If the person forced to retrieve a smash fears this stroke, he may hit several shots beyond the back line in an effort to keep the smasher in the rear of the court.

To be effective, the smash must be hit with proper form and accurately placed. Equally as important is knowing precisely *when* to smash. The thinking badminton player will play a series of shots that will eventually set up a smash which has a good chance of winning the point. Against good opposition, the smash should not be considered a means of winning the point outright. From a tactical standpoint, among experienced players, the smash is used as a means of making one's opponent *hit up*. This places the opponent on the defensive. If his return is weak, sometimes it can be put away; more often the reply is directed to a point in the opponent's court which forces an even weaker return. And following that, an even weaker one which may be struck away for the point.

## THE FOREHAND SMASH

The forehand smash—the most used of the smashes—is an overhead vertical stroke. Your body should be at a right angle to the net, with the left foot advanced. As the bird descends, weight is placed on the rear foot.

The head of the racket is cocked behind your head and right shoulder, with the racket held in an approximately horizontal position. As in all badminton strokes, the wrist is very important. Be sure to have it cocked as you await the descent of the bird.

*40*

At the proper moment, the body begins its turn to the right, the elbow is straightened, the right shoulder moves forward and weight is shifted from the right foot to the left. The arm rises to its full extension. The bird should be struck about a foot in front of the body. As the racket strikes the bird, with the full force of the arm, shoulder and body behind it, the wrist is brought sharply forward, adding whipping power to the stroke.

The feeling should be one of *covering* the bird—that is, hitting down on it and following through with the racket, bringing it down toward the floor. The direction

1

2

Smash

3

of the follow-through should be the same as the path the bird is traveling.

As the stroke is being made, the right foot will naturally be brought forward, so that weight will be mainly on it after completion of the stroke.

Concentration on the flight of the bird as it descends toward you is very important, since the eye has a tendency to be taken off the descending object at the last split second. For more accurate aim and also to help maintain balance prior to the stroke, you may find it useful to raise your left arm as you prepare to hit, virtually pointing at the bird. The arm is lowered in a natural manner as the body turn is made and the racket is brought up and over the bird.

Here are some faults players are apt to make in hitting the forehand smash:

(1) Failing to hit the smash steeply enough. If the bird goes far out into your opponent's court, it will be easier to retrieve.

(2) Hitting the smash with a bent elbow instead of a fully extended arm. This makes for a flat shot rather than a steep one—a shot that will go out of court or can be easily retrieved.

(3) Moving to the precise hitting position too late. The result of this can be hitting off balance or not getting the entire body behind the shot. In both cases, power is reduced.

(4) Smashing while moving backward. This, too, takes power from the shot and may cause the bird to go too far out in your opponent's court. If your opponent is alert, by using your own speed against you he may catch you off balance with his return.

(5) Jumping into the air to hit a smash. Beginners should not do it. The movement is tiring and the variation in height at which the bird is taken decreases the accuracy of the shot.

1

Round-the-head smash

2

3

## THE ROUND-THE-HEAD SMASH

This stroke, as the name implies, is made use of when the bird must be taken over the left shoulder of a right-handed player. (Two other strokes that might be made in this case are the high backhand—backhand smash—and the backhand drive. The round-the-head, if practiced diligently, is a much stronger shot.)

Stand more squarely to the net than for the conventional smash and bend your body toward the left. Your weight is mainly on the left foot. With the elbow sharply bent, the racket is carried behind the head and sweeps around it to make the stroke, the forearm brushing the

*43*

4

5

**Round-the-head smash**

6

top of the head before straightening. Because the wrist snap can be accentuated when the smash is made in this manner, the stroke is usually one of great severity.

Since there is a tendency—due to the pronounced wrist action—to propel the bird cross-court, you should practice hitting down the line as well. The shot is especially useful in attacking short, high shots that fall in the left side of the court and high serves that cannot be taken with the forehand smash.

## THE BACKHAND SMASH

This stroke is called a smash, but since the body cannot be put behind the shot (as in the forehand smash), the bird cannot be struck as forcibly. The bird is taken overhead on the left side of the body—the back being almost entirely turned to the net—and is hit with as much power as can be furnished by the outstretched arm and a fast downward and backward snapping of the wrist. It is a useful shot for attacking high, loose returns from the left-hand side of the court and should be part of every player's repertoire. Combined with the backhand overhead drop, it may win quite a few points.

## THE HALF-SMASH

Still another useful stroke is the half-smash—a forehand overhead shot that is somewhere between a full smash and a forehand overhead drop. It is hit when you do not wish to risk being placed off balance by making a full smash and when the overhead drop would not be effective.

A great deal of wrist and forearm is used in the shot to make the bird fall fast and steep, and the closer you can hit to the net tape, the better. The bird does not travel as far out in the court as when it is smashed, but does go farther out than the conventional overhead drop. When you first use it, do not try to hit close to the sidelines, but aim it toward the middle of the court. What is important is the shot's deceptiveness in flight—it is short for a smash but carries much greater descending speed than a drop. Because your opponent may be confused by its flight, he is apt to hit a weak return. The best time to use this shot is when your opponent is some distance from the net.

# 8
# Drop Shots and Net Shots

BECAUSE THE term "drop shot" is used by many players to include "net shots" as well as the various types of drop shots, it may be helpful to distinguish between the terms.

Drop shots are shots played from deep in the court, while net shots are shots played from points close to the net. Drop shots can be hit underhand or overhand, and ideally they cross the net by a tiny margin and drop steeply down into the opponent's court. Net shots are of two types: (1) shots hit delicately at a point near the net tape so that they barely cross in and drop quickly to the floor, or (2) shots hit sharply downward from a point slightly higher than the top of the net.

Drops, in all their forms, require the most delicate touch and the greatest wrist and finger control of all badminton shots. If hit properly and at the right time, they force your opponent to scramble forward, lunge for the bird and hit up—that is, they put him in a most vulnerable

*46*

Forehand overhead drop

defensive position. Mixed judiciously with clears, they are the most effective shots in the game for fatiguing an opponent.

## THE UNDERHAND DROP SHOT

This shot is made with a stroke similar to that for the underhand clear. On both forehand and backhand the bird is hit about a foot in front of the body, with the

**Backhand overhead drop**

racket controlled by the wrist and fingers. Because little power is desired, there is only a short follow-through. The grip is slightly looser than for the clear and you should hit *through* the bird, despite the fact that the stroke is a delicate one. Tapping the bird, as many players do in their effort not to hit it too hard, lessens control and the shot often goes in the net. The bird should be hit delicately but firmly, with the idea of making it soar swiftly through the air.

The underhand drop is effective in returning smashes, in tiring one's opponent by making him dash forward to retrieve it and in setting up openings for smashes should your opponent make a weak reply. It should be aimed to the spot on the court the greatest distance from your

4                                          5

opponent, since the farther he must travel, the nearer to the floor the shot will be by the time he reaches it.

## THE OVERHEAD DROP SHOT

On both forehand and backhand, the strokes for this shot should resemble those for the smash and the overhead clear—not only so the shot can be properly hit but to keep your opponent guessing until the last moment as to which type of stroke you are playing.

On the forehand, the position of the feet and body is similar to that for hitting an overhead clear. The bird should be struck as high in its flight as possible, and far enough in front of you so that the racket begins its downward arc at the moment of impact. This reduces the forward momentum you impart to the bird, and because of the bird's construction and conelike design it soon descends at a very steep angle. As with the underhand drop shots, the pronounced snap of the wrist is very important. There is little forward body movement and very little follow-through. *Some* follow-through is important, however, to make the action as smooth as possible. This smoothness can be attained if you develop the habit of hitting *through* the bird rather than *at* it.

On the forehand side, the overhead drop is an effective complement to the high clear and the smash. It is especially effective against a slow-footed or weary opponent, the shot being aimed to the point farthest away from him, compelling him to rush forward to retrieve a fast-descending object.

The position for hitting the overhead backhand drop shot is similar to that for hitting the overhead backhand clear—right foot forward, body turned so that the back is nearly facing the net. The bird is hit at a point as high above the body as can be comfortably reached and slightly in front of the right shoulder. Failure to turn sufficiently —that is, trying to hit the stroke with the body nearly square to the net—makes the shot very difficult, forcing the wrist to do a great deal more work than it should.

## NET SHOTS

The closer to the tape that these shots can be taken, the more effective they are. The earlier the bird can be reached and struck, of course, the better angle you have for hitting over the net. In hitting soft shots on both forehand and backhand, the body may be square to the net and the bird is *persuaded* over by delicate use of

Position of racket and bird in hitting a forehand net shot

the wrist. A very slight turn of the wrist suffices to direct the bird where you wish it to go. It should be hit lightly enough barely to cross the net and it should fall steeply to the floor almost immediately afterward. Be careful not to strike the net with your racket, as this will cost you the point.

The net shot is valuable as an outright point winner or as a means of forcing your opponent to make an underhand reply. The reply—an ineffectual drop shot or short lob—may be weak enough to be smashed for the point.

If the bird is taken at tape height or higher, it should be directed toward an open spot in your opponent's court. If the bird is taken lower, the best shot is usually along the net, which has the effect of lengthening the flight and flattening the angle. Also, the fact that the bird is traveling

Position of racket and bird in hitting a backhand net shot

along the net ensures that it will not go deep into your opponent's court and give him an easy return.

When the opportunity offers, another type of net shot is one that is sharply hit and aimed steeply downward to an open part of your opponent's court. It is a shot used most often in doubles, where one partner is stationed at the net primarily for the purpose of putting away loose shots.

If such a weak shot is seen approaching, it is advisable to move in rapidly and take it high and as close to the net tape as is consistent with safety. The least hesitation in attacking this type of shot makes it immensely more difficult to place the bird where your opponent cannot reach it.

# 9
# Drives

THE DRIVE off the forehand and backhand is a shot hit flat and kept as low as possible in relation to the net. It is a stroke which is not practiced or used enough in badminton.

This is not an easy shot to master because a great deal of power must be imparted when the shot is hit from the back of the court and, for this, proper footwork is essential. If the feet are not placed correctly, a strain is placed on the shoulder and the forearm. Any unnatural motion used in hitting the drive will result in inaccurate shots and unnecessary fatigue. A common fault of players in hitting the drive is preparing late and striking the bird after it has passed the body, so that a kind of arm and wrist contortion is required to keep the bird in the opponent's court.

Despite the comparative difficulty of execution, the drive, properly hit, is a most effective stroke. It is useful in both singles and mixed doubles to keep an opponent running from side to side (in mixed doubles, it is the

Forehand drive

male player who is kept running). The drive must always be hit at peak speed and kept flat. Since it is without loft, it must arrive at the end of its flight as quickly as possible; otherwise it is vulnerable to being struck by the opponent, if he has time to get to it, the moment it crosses the net.

A quick-driven stroke is also effective if your opponent is close to the net and the shot is aimed directly at him, cramping his return. Finally, it is a very effective reply to a smash by your opponent in the event that the smash comes too far out into your court. If your opponent is off-balance after the smash, the quickly driven low return may force a weak reply.

3

4

## THE FOREHAND DRIVE

For the necessary power when hitting drives from the back of the court (where they will be struck at about knee height and have a rising trajectory), the left foot must be placed in front of the right and farther over toward the right sideline than the right foot.

As you draw the racket back in preparation for the shot, with the elbow bent and the wrist cocked, your body should turn so that at the finish of the backswing your back is toward the net. Both knees should be bent—the left more than the right—and weight placed on the rear

**Backhand drive**

foot. As the bird approaches, the racket is rapidly brought
forward as the elbow straightens for the shot, the body
pivots, weight is transferred from the rear to the front
foot and, just before the bird is struck, the wrist sharply
uncocks. The bird should be struck at a point about a
foot in front of the body. There is a long follow-through
in the direction of the line of flight of the bird, leaving
you facing the net and ready for your opponent's return.

Less preparation is necessary (or possible) when the
bird is taken about halfway up the court. The body is at
right angles to the net and the feet are approximately
parallel to the sideline. Here the bird is struck at about
waist height and the bend of the left knee is not so
pronounced.

56

3

4

If a quick-driven shot is made quite near the net, it should be hit as near the level of the tape as possible (as opposed to taking the bird late and relatively low) and only a slight twist of the body is necessary for the power needed. In this case, the racket must be held quite firmly. In some instances, as when you have intercepted a fast shot, the speed of your return is determined by the force of your opponent's shot.

## THE BACKHAND DRIVE

From the back of the court, necessary power is put into the stroke by placing the right foot closer to the left sideline than the left foot, turning the body so that the back

57

faces the net, bending the right knee and bringing the racket far back at about hip level. The elbow and the forearm make nearly a 90-degree angle and the wrist is sharply cocked. As the uncoiling motion starts, the arm is straightened, weight is put on the right foot and, just before the bird is struck, the wrist uncocks. The bird should be hit about a foot in front of the body. If it is struck early in its flight, the shot will go cross-court; if it is taken later, the shot will go down the line. At the conclusion of the stroke, the racket arm should be fairly high and fully extended. The force behind the stroke places the body square to the net, ready for the opponent's reply.

If the bird is taken halfway up the court, the right foot should be placed in line with the left, the body twisting to the left as the backhand grip is assumed. Little power can be put into the shot if the body does not pivot.

If a driven shot must be made quite near the net, the right shoulder moves slightly to the left as the racket is drawn back, but the body remains square to the net. Power and direction for the shot are supplied by a firm thumb, the wrist and the forward movement of the arm.

# 10
# Singles Tactics

IN NO racket game does defense change to offense so rapidly as in badminton, and the attacker can lose the offensive equally fast. A single return, well hit, will drive your opponent back and force him to reply with a defensive shot; or a drop shot off a smash may have him scrambling to get his racket on the bird. By the same token, you may see an opening for a point—but your opponent, having anticipated the shot, has made a forcing return and has now got *you* in trouble.

In badminton rallies, there is constant planning, constant searching for an opening, constant probing for weaknesses. To become more effective in this mental duel with your opponent, you must learn certain fundamental tactics of the game—otherwise, condition and stroking skill will not count for much. The successful badminton player is one who has a definite purpose behind every shot he makes.

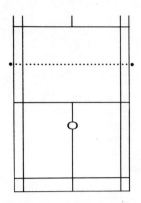

In singles, position indicated by circle is where players should return after hitting a shot.

## SERVING

The high serve is most frequently used so that full advantage can be taken of the length of the receiver's half court. At the beginning of a match, serve high and deep, aiming the bird to fall between the two back lines. If you find you are hitting out, correct this by hitting the bird later in your swing and in a more nearly vertical direction, still using the full power stroke. If your serve is falling short, presenting your opponent with an easy smash, hit the bird earlier in your swing but see that its flight is not quite so vertical. Again, use the full power stroke. As the game progresses and you find your touch, your objective should be to serve so that the bird, if allowed to drop, would fall within a few inches of the baseline.

Unless your opponent has an extremely hard smash and is able to place the bird within an inch or two of the sidelines, he will be unlikely to hit an outright winner; and even if he is able to, the effort involved in constant smashing will soon tire him. A deep serve also makes it more difficult for him to reply with an accurate overhead drop.

The low serve is used about 10 per cent of the time and most often should be directed toward the left front corner of your opponent's right half court and the right front corner of his left half court, as mentioned in Chapter 5.

Your serves, of course, should be constantly altered so that your opponent will not know what to expect—high ones mixed with low ones, serves sent wide as well as to the interior sections of the half courts. Occasionally the flick serve should be directed over your opponent's head if you think he expects a low serve, and the drive serve should be hit right at his upper chest if you think it will take him by surprise.

## RECEIVING SERVES

Unless your opponent has a very weak low serve, you should not rush it in singles. If you do so, his reply to your return probably will be a sharp flick over your head and you will have to scramble back to reach it. In doubles, of course, you have a partner to make such retrieves.

If your opponent's low serves are well placed, your best reply is a deep underhand clear—most of the time to his backhand corner—which chases him to the back of the court.

A high serve of good length should usually be returned with an overhead clear; one of poor length should usually be smashed. These returns should be varied with overhead drops so that your opponent can never be sure where to expect the return. If your opponent is serving high and deep and seems to have no problem in returning your smashes, you should forsake this reply for something less fatiguing. If you do not, you are likely to become weary before the game is over and your accuracy will suffer.

## RALLIES

A mistake many players make at the beginning of a match is the assumption that their shots are going to go precisely where they aim them. On certain shots—smashes, drives and drops—you should allow a reasonable margin of safety at the start. This can range from 8 inches for drops to several feet in the case of smashes. While you may be reducing your effectiveness somewhat, at least you will not be giving away early, morale-building points to your opponent by hitting out.

A simple and sound strategy for beginning players to adopt is to alternate clears and drop shots, supplementing this tactic with smashes and drives as openings occur. Clearing close to the back line and dropping close to the net forces your opponent to race back and forth to make his returns and tends to fatigue him. Also, this is the kind of game that is difficult for him to break up.

Should your opponent utilize the same strategy, you should try to place him on the defensive, replying to his clear with a drop shot—not with a clear. The drop will force him up to the net. If he replies to your drop with a drop, you should clear; if he clears, you should reply with another drop. In the last case, however, if your drop has brought him so close to the net that he will have difficulty getting back, hit a clear.

After every shot, you should try to return to your base—a position on the middle line, a little closer to the net than to the back line (see diagram, p. 60), which allows you most easily to meet all the possible replies of your opponent. Many beginning players do not return to this position quickly enough—or fail to hit shots that enable them to reach it comfortably. These shots include those that allow you to remain on balance after the stroke, shots that have you moving in the direction in which you

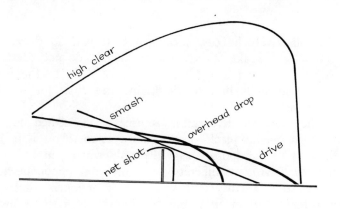

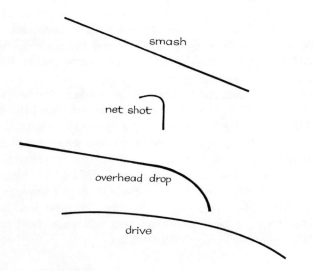

Various types of badminton shots

wish to go and clears that afford you the time you need to get there.

At the start of play, test your opponent—see if his backhand is weak or if he prefers to hit low rather than high shots. Determine how well he returns smashes and drives, how effectively he covers the court. If you do discern a pronounced weakness—say, the backhand—do not attack it without proper preparation. Hit a shot deep to the forehand that pulls him to the right, and *then* hit to the backhand.

The most effective smash is usually one aimed out of your opponent's reach—but a good rule to follow is to hit these shots (and drops as well) only when you feel you can reach without difficulty any reply your opponent may make. After a cross-court smash, your opponent probably will reply with a drop toward the corner farthest away from the point from which you hit the smash. If you are off balance, you may find the drop hard to reach. A smash hit straight down the court, by contrast, is easier for your opponent to retrieve in most cases, and his reply, likewise, probably will be straight down the court—a shot which you can reach more easily.

The most important thing to remember during rallies is: *Be patient*. Against a worthy opponent, you will have to hit stroke after stroke to make your opening, and the most futile thing you can do is to toss away a point by aiming too close to a line and hitting out or aiming too close to the top of the net and failing to clear it. Plan your shots, learn to spot the openings (don't go for them before they are there), develop the ability to place the bird where you wish—and you will soon be beating players more experienced than you are.

# 11
# Doubles

DOUBLES IS played a great deal more than singles in badminton, and many players find it a more enjoyable game. Youth and stamina are not at such a premium and the tactical aspects are engrossing—but mistakes are severely and promptly punished.

In all three types of doubles—men's, ladies' and mixed —the basic tactics are the same:

(1) Hit shots that will allow your partner to use his best strokes.

(2) Try to gain the attack (that is, make your opponents hit up) and hold it.

(3) Try to control the net.

(4) Put pressure on the server by rushing low serves and smashing high ones.

In doubles, where court coverage is not nearly the problem it is in singles, points are generally won by hitting fast, accurate shots, and the tempo is much faster than in singles. Anticipation of shots and the aggressive interception of shots are extremely important.

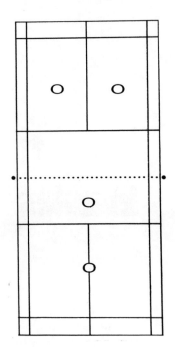

Doubles positions indicated are (top) side-by-side (defensive) and (bottom) up-and-back (offensive).

There are two main doubles formations: side-by-side and up-and-back. In side-by-side doubles, the court is divided into two halves, with one partner taking everything on his side and the other partner covering the rest of the court. Shots down the middle are generally received by the player on the left side, since he can take them on his forehand. This formation is useful for defense but not for attack.

The up-and-back position is taken when a team is attacking. One partner is posted at the net, ready to kill loose shots, and the other is behind him, ready to deal with anything that the player at the net cannot reach.

A good low serve is of primary importance in all types of doubles; indeed, in an even match the disparity in the effectiveness of low serves of the players may be the de-

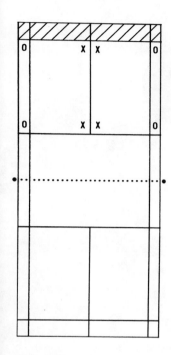

Most effective aim points for serve in doubles: X—best; O—next best

ciding factor. A player with a good low serve is the best kind of partner, while one with a weak low serve may cost his team fully half the number of points it should have taken.

In serving to the first court, the best aim point is the area close to the center line and the front service line. This will not necessarily produce a winner, but the receiver cannot hit an attacking shot off it. A low serve that falls to the extreme outer edge of the court can be effective, but if your opponent sees it coming and reaches it early, he may be able to place it in an open spot in your court. In serving to the second court, you should usually aim toward your opponent's forehand corner.

Your lob serve, when you make use of it, must be very deep and quite high to avoid giving the receiver an easy

In mixed doubles, position of lady player at the net

smash. Its primary functions are to catch the receiver off guard when he is expecting a low serve and to keep him from consistently rushing in to attack your low serve. The best place to aim it is deep to the receiver's backhand in the first court and deep to the receiver's forehand in the second court. Keeping the bird deep and in the middle of the court cuts down the angle of the smasher's possible replies.

In all doubles, the receiver should rush the low serve at every opportunity, one of the purposes being to shake the confidence of the server. This involves standing as close to the net as the service court permits—but the receiver should be alert to hurry back in the court in the event that a high serve is used to surprise him.

The best position of readiness for rushing a low serve is to stand with the left foot advanced and the knee slightly bent. The weight is placed on the left foot, with the right foot ready to start the body forward. The racket is high and held in the "flat," or Western, grip. As the serve is hit, the receiver pushes off toward the net with his right foot and moves the racket forward. The object of the receiver is to reach the bird quickly—before it has had a chance to descend after crossing the net—and hit sharply down with a kind of jabbing motion. This stance also allows the receiver to move backward quickly in the event that the lob serve is hit. High serves should be taken on the forehand as much as possible.

Position of receiver in anticipation of a low serve in doubles

Side-by-side (defensive) position in doubles

The basic doubles tactic during an attack is for the partner of the player hitting down to move forward and cover the net, where he can put away any loose replies. If the opposing team replies with a deep clear, the player at the net stays there, since his team has been given the attack. He moves back when his partner hits a clear and after he hits a clear himself.

It is a mistake, however, to come too close to the net on your partner's drops or smashes; the best place to stand is just ahead of the front service line. The partner who has hit the smash or drop should then take a position in the center of the court, about 4 feet inside the back line.

Even more than in singles, the winner in doubles is the

70

side that maintains the attack. Timidity does not pay off in doubles, where the nature of the game permits players to take many risks on the chance that they can put away a shot. The venturesome player, if he should make a miscalculation, can often be covered by his partner.

After serving, the server can do one of two things: (1) move up to handle any net shots the receiver may make, or (2) remain where he is. If he moves up, his partner takes a position on the middle line about 4 feet from the baseline. If he remains in place, his partner comes forward and shares responsibility for the shots close to the net.

It is probably best for the beginning player to remain

where he is after serving, since the receiver may hit a reply off the serve that will be difficult to get back. As mastery of the low serve increases, however, the server can come forward more aggressively.

When a high serve is delivered, the server and his partner take up the side-by-side position, the server moving backward after serving and his partner moving forward while the serve is in the air. This position is taken because it is assumed that the receiver will place his team on the attack by smashing the high serve. Each player on the serving team covers half the court and shares responsibility for covering net shots.

A frequent reply to the short serve is a clear deep to the serving team's backhand corner, which theoretically puts the serving team on the attack, although this is often a difficult shot to return.

The drop shot and smash should be used a great deal to maintain a constant attack. The lob, on the other hand, should be used only to gain time when either you or your partner are out of position. The more accurate your drop

**Up-and-back (offensive) position in doubles**

shot is, the better chance you have of forcing your opponents to lob, enabling you to hit smashes.

If your opponents have a weak defense, you should smash frequently, even if you leave openings while doing it. However, if they play well defensively, you should hit fewer smashes and more drops. Smashes should be hit steeply and aimed, if no opening presents itself, down the middle, since your opponents may be undecided as to which one should take a particular shot. This applies to drops also.

If your opponents are out of position, aim for the uncovered part of the court as a means of winning the point or forcing a weak return. If they are *in* position, try to make an extremely accurate, fast stroke or a drop shot that barely clears the net and drops steeply down.

In mixed doubles, the up-and-back formation is the most advantageous one to use. The woman stays at the net, ready to make put-aways, while the man stays back, hitting strokes like the smash, the drop and the drive. All these strokes force underhand replies, if hit properly, and provide the woman with the opportunity of cutting off the opposing

side's shots at the net. The man uses the clear—which must be hit very deep—only when he requires time to return to his base.

The woman may not be able to smash as severely as the man or hit deep clears as easily, but at the net she is likely to be as quick and aggressive as her partner. She should stand in the center of the court, just in front of the short service line, accepting responsibility for shots that come near the net throughout its entire width. She should not stand too close to the net, however, as that tends to cramp her movements. On the other hand, she should not be too far away, since she may obstruct her partner's view of the bird. Because of the kind of shots she will be hitting, she should hold the racket in the flat grip—the grip also used for rushing low serves. The racket should be held at the level of the net tape.

If she or her partner hits a high clear, she should bend down so that her face is below the level of the tape and is therefore protected from the smashes of opponents. Her racket should be held level with the net tape so that she will be able to hit back any shot that comes near.

Besides covering the back of the court, the male player in mixed doubles must be ready to come to the aid of his partner when she is out of position. An example of this assistance is dashing forward to retrieve a drop when the woman player cannot reach it. In such a case, he should hit a high, deep lob to allow his partner and himself to get back in position. Any other reply probably will result in an opponent's hitting a flick shot that will go over his head.

At net, the woman should try to make shots that force her opponents to hit up, enabling her partner to smash or hit overhead drops. She should avoid pushing the bird out into her opponents' court, but instead should drop it back just over the net. She should not loft a clear unless she sees a definite opening. If she has a chance to hit the bird down steeply, she should do so rather than hit a drop shot. The

74

fast-traveling steep shot will be difficult for the opponents to reach, and even if the point is not won outright the reply probably will be a weak lob that can be smashed.

Most of the woman player's shots should be net shots, aimed close to the top of the net and toward open spots in the opponents' court. Her follow-through on these shots should be checked, however, for two reasons: (1) so that the racket will be ready for a possible quick reply and (2) to make sure that the racket does not hit the net. (You may bring the racket over the net after hitting the bird on your side, but you are not allowed to touch the net with any part of the racket or body.)

Occasionally the woman may help defend against smashes, but this requires very fast reflexes. In most cases, she should let her partner handle the retrieving when the pair are caught in the up-and-back formation; the man should try to make openings for his partner and keep her, as much as possible, from having to return difficult shots. He should try to make his male opponent cover a great deal of court and avoid exposing his partner to smashes.

For a woman, the short, low serve is best, although the high one should be used occasionally. This is not only a surprise but is very effective when delivered to the opposing female player as a means of forcing her back in the court and away from her base at the net. This stratagem is not used enough. The short serve, conversely, brings the male player to the net, where he does not want to be.

Partners can help each other a great deal by shouting "Out!" or "No!" when they see the striker on their side about to hit a shot that would fall beyond the line if left alone. The person not striking usually has a better view of this than the striker. In most cases, the woman should not turn around while her partner is hitting behind her lest she be struck by the bird on a low shot. When the bird is hit far to the side or far to the rear of the court by the opposing side, she can risk turning to help her partner decide whether to let the bird fall to the floor or return it.

75

# 12
# Practice

BADMINTON IS a game requiring an extremely delicate touch. It is also a game in which reflexes must be very sharp. In singles particularly, unless strokes are made properly, fatigue inevitably will set in and coordination and accuracy will suffer. The greatest tactician in the world cannot play good badminton if his touch is off and if he cannot make the bird go where he wants it to.

Because of this, it is safe to say that practice in badminton is at least as important as practice in any other sport. You cannot improve stroke fundamentals during a match, and a sense of touch will not magically come just because you have need of it. Perfecting badminton strokes requires a good deal of work, patience and concentration.

There are two worthwhile ways to practice shots. The first is by yourself—against a wall, preferably one with a line on it the same height as the net (5 feet above the floor). For best results, a standard tournament bird with feathers and a cork base should be used, although any type of indoor bird is good.

By hitting the bird against the wall, you can practice clears on both forehand and backhand, smashes, overhead drops, underhand drops and serves. Hitting strokes in this manner for about half an hour a day or more will improve your reflexes, strengthen your wrist and accustom you to changing your grip rapidly. It will also help in learning to anticipate where the next shot is coming and force you to move quickly around for shots with a minimum of steps. Practicing in this way will improve stamina, too. (Hitting against two walls at right angles to each other, so that you can practice changing the direction of your shots, is even better.)

Here are some of the things to concentrate on while hitting against a wall or two walls:

(1) Quickly change the grip from backhand to forehand and vice versa so that the movement becomes an automatic reflex.

(2) Make full use of the wrist on shots where a great deal of wrist is required and practice hitting the bird delicately when making drop shots.

(3) Aim for consistency—try not to miss.

(4) Get the racket back in plenty of time, in most cases as you move into position for the shot.

(5) Pay special attention to footwork, trying to reach the bird in as few steps as possible while maintaining good balance. In practicing shots where power is called for, make sure the body is properly pivoted.

(6) In serving, try to develop wrist snap and smoothness of motion for the high serves; aim low serves just over the line representing the net.

In practicing with an opponent—a player as desirous as you are to improve strokes and confidence—there are two important mental attitudes you should adopt. First, you should have a definite purpose to the practice. Set up a

specific program so that you can concentrate on certain shots without wasting any time. And, second, do not be easily satisfied. Do not assume that you have perfected a shot because you have hit it well, say, five times. The higher the standard you set, the more rapid will be your progress. Can you hit it well twenty-five times? Thirty?

Here is a recommended program of practice against an opponent. It is divided into two sessions, since it is difficult to practice all the various shots efficiently in a single session. Several birds are used.

## FIRST SESSION (HALF HOUR)

(1) After a five-minute warm-up of batting the bird back and forth, the players move forward and hit delicate underhand net shots to each other. The shots can go straight over the net or along the length of the net. They should be aimed to clear the tape by an inch or so and fall quickly on the other side. Emphasis is on touch and developing wrist and finger control. *About 3 minutes.*

(2) One player smashes while his opponent replies with clears. After 3 minutes, the players reverse roles. (Players should not overdo the full smash, as this can be quite tiring.) *Total of 6 minutes.*

(3) One player hits clears to the backhand corner while his opponent replies with the backhand overhead drop. After 4 minutes, the roles are reversed. *Total of 8 minutes.*

(4) One player hits clears to the forehand corner while his opponent replies with the forehand overhead drop. After 4 minutes, the roles are reversed. *Total of 8 minutes.*

## SECOND SESSION (HALF HOUR)

(1) After a five-minute warm-up, one player hits high serves to his opponent's forehand and backhand which are

80

returned by smashes. (Birds are not retrieved.) After 3 minutes, the roles are reversed. *Total of 6 minutes.*

(2) One player hits low serves to the left and right sides of each court of his opponent. Serves are rushed by receiver, using the flat grip and trying to meet the serve early and hit it sharply down. (Birds are not retrieved.) After 4 minutes, the players reverse roles. *Total of 8 minutes.*

(3) One player smashes; opponent returns with underhand drop. (Birds are not retrieved.) After 2 minutes, roles are reversed. *Total of 4 minutes.*

(4) Each player stands at midcourt and they exchange drives, hit hard and aimed low. These drives can be aimed down the lines, cross-court or at the chest of the player on the other side of the net. *About 3 minutes.*

(5) Players alternate hitting clears and drops—basic singles tactics—for 4 minutes, trying to keep the rallies going as long as possible.


A player who has a particular weakness may wish to spend more time trying to correct it instead of going over those shots at which he is proficient. Shots which give most beginners trouble are: the low serve (going too high over the net), the high serve (not going deep enough), the clear (not deep enough) and the smash (going too far out in the opponent's court).

It is a good idea, even if you play doubles principally, to indulge in an occasional game of singles. This will increase your stamina and will probably point out some weaknesses you may have which are not so obvious in the doubles game. Also, it is advisable—as in all sports—to play as much as possible with somebody better than you are. By doing this, you will learn how rapidly you must move around the court against good opposition, how accurate your shots must be, how quickly you must think under pressure and how hard it is to earn points against a reasonably skillful player.

# 13
# The Laws
# of Badminton

1. (a) COURT—The court shall be laid out as in the diagram on page 16 (except in the case provided for in paragraph "b" of this Law) and to the measurements there shown and shall be defined by white, black or other easily distinguishable lines, 1½ inches wide.

In marking the court, the width (1½ inches) of the center lines shall be equally divided between the right and left service-courts; the width (1½ inches each) of the short service line and the long service line shall fall within the 13 foot measurement given as the length of the service-court; and the width (1½ inches each) of all other boundary lines shall fall within the measurements given.

(b) Where space does not permit of the marking out of a court for doubles, a court may be marked out for singles (see the same diagram on page 16). The back boundary lines become also the long service lines (doubles long service line omitted), and the posts, or the strips of material representing them as referred to in Law 2, shall be placed on the side lines.

2. POSTS—The posts shall be 5 feet 1 inch in height from the floor. They shall be sufficiently firm to keep the net strained as provided in Law 3, and shall be placed on the side boundary lines of the court. Where this is not practicable, some method must be employed for indicating the position of the side boundary line where it passes under the net, e.g., by the use of a thin post or strip of material, not less than 1½ inches in width, fixed to the side boundary line and rising vertically to the net cord. Where this is in use on a court marked for doubles it shall be placed on the side boundary line of the doubles court irrespective of whether singles or doubles are being played.

3. NET—The net shall be made of fine tanned cord of ¼ inch mesh. It shall be firmly stretched from post to post, and shall be 2 feet 6 inches in depth. The top of the net shall be 5 feet in height from the floor at the center, and 5 feet 1 inch at the posts, and shall be edged with a 3 inch white tape doubled and supported by a cord or cable run through the tape and strained over and flush with the top of the posts.

4. SHUTTLE—A shuttle shall weigh from 73 to 85 grains, and shall have from 14 to 16 feathers fixed in a cork, 1 inch to 1⅛ inches in diameter. The feathers shall be from 2½ to 2¾ inches in length from the tip to the top of the cork base. They shall have from 2⅜ to 2½ inches spread at the top and shall be firmly fastened with thread or other suitable material.

Subject to there being no substantial variation in the general design, pace, weight and flight of the shuttle, modifications in the above specifications may be made, subject

84

to the approval of the National Organization concerned (a) in places where atmospheric conditions, due either to altitude or climate, make the standard shuttle unsuitable; or (b) if special circumstances exist which make it otherwise expedient in the interests of the game.

A shuttle shall be deemed to be of correct pace if, when a player of average strength strikes it with a full underhand stroke from a spot immediately above one back boundary line in a line parallel to the side lines, and at an upward angle, it falls not less than 1 foot, and not more than 2 feet 6 inches, short of the other back boundary line.

5. (a) PLAYERS—The word "player" applies to all those taking part in a game.

(b) The game shall be played, in the case of the doubles game, by two players a side, and in the case of the singles game, by one player a side.

(c) The side for the time being having the right to serve shall be called the "in" side, and the opposing side shall be called the "out" side.

6. TOSS—Before commencing play the opposing sides shall toss, and the side winning the toss shall have the option of:—(a) Serving first; or (b) Not serving first; (c) Choosing ends. The side losing the toss shall then have choice of any alternative remaining.

7. (a) SCORING—The doubles and men's singles game consists of 15 or 21 points, as may be arranged. Provided that in a game of 15 points, when the score is 13-all, the side which first reached 13 has the option of "setting" the game to 5, and that when the score is 14-all, the side which first reached 14 has the option of "setting" the game to 3. After a game has been "set" the score is called "love-all," and the side which first scores 5 or 3 points, according as the game

has been "set" at 13- or 14-all, wins the game. In either case the claim to "set" the game must be made before the next service is delivered after the score has reached 13-all or 14-all. Provided also that in a game of 21 points the same method of scoring be adopted, substituting 19 and 20 for 13 and 14.

(b) The ladies' single game consists of 11 points. Provided that when the score is "9-all" the player who first reached 9 has the option of "setting" the game to 3, and when the score is "10-all" the player who first reached 10 has the option of "setting" the game to 2.

(c) A side rejecting the option of "setting" at the first opportunity shall not be thereby debarred from "setting" if a second opportunity arises.

(d) In handicap games "setting" is not permitted.

8. The opposing sides shall contest the best of 3 games, unless otherwise agreed. The players shall change ends at the commencement of the second game and also of the third game (if any). In the third game the players shall change ends when the leading score reaches:—

(a) 8 in a game of 15 points;

(b) 6 in a game of 11 points;

(c) 11 in a game of 21 points;

or, in handicap events, when one of the sides has scored half the total number of points required to win the game (the next highest number being taken in case of fractions). When it has been agreed to play only one game the players shall change ends as provided above for the third game.

If, inadvertently, the players omit to change ends as provided in this Law at the score indicated, the ends shall be changed immediately the mistake is discovered, and the existing score shall stand.

9. (a) DOUBLES PLAY—It having been decided which side is to have the service, the player in the right-hand service-court of that side commences the game by serving to the player in the service-court diagonally opposite. If the latter player returns the shuttle before it touches the ground, it is to be returned by one of the "in" side, and then returned by one of the "out" side, and so on, till a fault is made or the shuttle ceases to be "in play" (see paragraph (b)). If a fault is made by the "in" side, its right to continue serving is lost, as only one player on the side beginning a game is entitled to do so (vide Law 11), and the opponent in the right-hand service-court then becomes the server; but if the service is not returned, or the fault is made by the "out" side, the "in" side scores a point. The "in" side players then change from one service-court to the other, the service now being from the left-hand service-court to the player in the service-court diagonally opposite. So long as a side remains "in," service is delivered alternately from each service-court into the one diagonally opposite, the change being made by the "in" side when, and only when a point is added to its score.

(b) The first service of a side in each inning shall be made from the right-hand service-court. A "service" is delivered as soon as the shuttle is struck by the server's racket. The shuttle is thereafter "in play" until it touches the ground, or until a fault or "let" occurs, or except as provided in Law 19. After the service is delivered, the server and the player served to may take up any position they choose on their side of the net, irrespective of any boundary lines.

10. The player served to may alone receive the service, but should the shuttle touch, or be struck by, his partner the "in" side scores a point. No player may receive two consecutive services in the same game, except as provided in Law 12.

11. Only one player of the side beginning a game shall be entitled to serve in its first innings. In all subsequent innings, each partner shall have the right, and they shall serve consecutively. The side winning a game shall always serve first in the next game, but either of the winners may serve and either of the losers may receive the service.

12. If a player serves out of turn, or from the wrong service-court (owing to a mistake as to the service-court from which service is at the time being in order), *and his side wins the rally*, it shall be a "let," provided that such "let" be claimed or allowed before the next succeeding service is delivered.

If a player standing in the wrong service-court takes the service, *and his side wins the rally*, it shall be a "let," provided that such "let" be claimed or allowed before the next succeeding service is delivered. If in either of the above cases the side at fault *loses the rally*, the mistake shall stand and the players' position shall not be corrected during the remainder of that game.

Should a player inadvertently change sides when he should not do so and the mistake not be discovered until after the next succeeding service has been delivered, the mistake shall stand, and a "let" cannot be claimed or allowed, and the players' position shall not be corrected during the remainder of that game.

13. SINGLES PLAY—In singles Laws 9 to 12 hold good except that:—

(a) The players shall serve from the receive service in their respective right-hand service-courts only when the server's score is 0 or an even number of points in the game, the service being delivered from and received in their respective left-hand service-courts when the server's score is an odd number of points.

(b) Both players shall change service-courts after each point has been scored.

14. FAULTS—A fault made by a player of the side which is "in" puts the server out; if made by a player whose side is "out," it counts a point to the "in" side.

It is a fault:—

(a) If, in serving, the shuttle at the instant of being struck be higher than the server's waist, or if any part of the head of the racket, at the instant of striking the shuttle, be higher than any part of the server's hand holding the racket.

(b) If, in serving, the shuttle falls into the wrong service-court, (i.e., into the one not diagonally opposite to the server), or falls short of the short service line, or beyond the long service line, or outside the side boundary lines of the service-court into which service is in order.

(c) If the server's feet are not in the service-court from which service is at the time being in order, or if the feet of the player receiving the service are not in the service-court diagonally opposite until the service is delivered. (See Law 16.)

(d) If before or during the delivery of the service any player makes preliminary feints or otherwise intentionally balks his opponent, or if any player deliberately delays serving the shuttle, or in getting ready to receive it, so as to obtain an unfair advantage.

(e) If, either in service or play, the shuttle falls outside the boundaries of the court, or passes through or under the net, or fails to pass the net, or touches the roof or side walls, or the person or dress of a player. (A shuttle falling on a line shall be deemed to have fallen in the court or service-court of which such line is a boundary.)

(f) If the shuttle "in play" be struck before it crosses to the striker's side of the net. (The striker may, however, follow the shuttle over the net with his racket in the course of his stroke.

(g) If, when the shuttle is "in play," a player touches the net or its supports with racket, person or dress.

(h) If the shuttle be held on the racket (i.e., caught or slung) during the execution of a stroke; or if the shuttle be hit twice in succession by the same player with two strokes; or if the shuttle be hit by a player and his partner successively.

(i) If in play a player strikes the shuttle (unless he thereby makes a good return) or is struck by it, whether he is standing within or outside the boundaries of the court.

(j) If a player obstructs an opponent.

(k) If Law 16 be transgressed.

15. GENERAL—The server may not serve till his opponent is ready, but the opponent shall be deemed to be ready if a return of the service be attempted.

16. The server and the player served to must stand within the limits of their respective service-courts (as bounded by the short and long service, the center, and side lines), and some part of both feet of these players must remain in contact with the ground in a stationary position until the service is delivered. A foot on or touching a line in the case of either the server or the receiver shall be held to be outside his service-court. (See Law 14(c).) The respective partners may take up any position, provided they do not unsight or otherwise obstruct an opponent.

17. If, in the course of service or rally, the shuttle touches and passes over the net, the stroke is not invalidated

thereby. It is a good return if the shuttle, having passed outside either post, drops on or within the boundary lines of the opposite court. A "let" may be given by the umpire, for any unforeseen or accidental hindrance. If, in service, or during a rally, a shuttle, after passing over the net, is caught in or on the net, it is a "let." If the receiver is faulted for moving before the service is delivered, or for not being within the correct service-court, in accordance with Laws 14 (c) or 16, and at the same time the server is also faulted for a service infringement, it shall be a "let." When a "let" occurs, the play since the last service shall not count, and the player who served shall serve again.

18. If the server, in attempting to serve, miss the shuttle, it is not a fault; but if the shuttle be touched by the racket, a service is thereby delivered.

19. If, when in play, the shuttle strikes the net and remains suspended there, or strikes the net and falls towards the surface of the court on the striker's side of the net, or hits the surface outside the court and an opponent then touches the net or shuttle with his racket or person, there is no penalty, as the shuttle is not *then* in play.

20. If a player has a chance of striking the shuttle in a downward direction when quite near the net, his opponent must not put up his racket near the net on the chance of the shuttle rebounding from it.

This is obstruction within the meaning of Law 14(j).

A player may, however, hold up his racket to protect his face from being hit if he does not thereby balk his opponent.

21. It shall be the duty of the umpire to call "fault" or "let" should either occur, without appeal being made by the players, and to give his decision on any appeal regarding a point in dispute, if made before the next service; and also

to appoint linesmen and service judges at his discretion. The umpire's decision shall be final, but he shall uphold the decision of a linesman or service judge. This does not preclude the umpire also from faulting the server or receiver. Where, however, a referee is appointed, an appeal shall lie to him from the decision of an umpire on questions of law only.

22. Play shall be continuous from the first service until the match be concluded: except that (a) in the International Badminton Championships and in the Ladies' International Championships, there shall be allowed an interval not exceeding five minutes between the second and third games of a match; (b) in countries where climatic conditions render it desirable, there shall be allowed, subject to the previously published approval of the National Organization concerned, an interval not exceeding five minutes between the second and third games of a match, in singles or doubles, or both, and (c) when necessitated by circumstances not within the control of the players, the umpire may suspend play for such period as he may consider necessary. If play be suspended, the existing score shall stand and play be resumed from that point. Under no circumstances shall play be suspended to enable a player to recover his strength or wind, or to receive instruction or advice. Except in the case of any interval already provided for above, no player shall be allowed to leave the court until the match be concluded without the umpire's consent. The umpire shall be the sole judge of any suspension of play and he shall have the right to disqualify an offender. (In the U.S., at the request of any player, a five-minute rest period between the 2nd and 3rd game will be granted, in all events. Such a rest period is mandatory for all Junior Tournaments.)

# INTERPRETATIONS

1. Any movement or conduct by the server that has the effect of breaking the continuity of service after the server and receiver have taken their positions to serve and to receive the service is a preliminary feint. For example, a server who, after having taken up his position to serve, delays hitting the shuttle for so long as to be unfair to the receiver, is guilty of such conduct. (See Law 14(d).) Note: U.S.A. interpretation is it is a fault if the serve is not delivered in 5 seconds from the time that both server and receiver have taken their stance.

2. It is obstruction if a player invade an opponent's court with racket or person in any degree except as permitted in Law 14(f). (See Law 14(j).)

3. Where necessary on account of the structure of a building, the local Badminton Authority may, subject to the right of veto of its National Organization, make by-laws dealing with cases in which a shuttle touches an obstruction.

These rules may change from year to year to some extent. Hence, to assure yourself that you are dealing with the up-to-date rules, secure them from:

Lester E. Hilton, Chairman
ABA Rules Committee
15 Tanglewood Drive
Cumberland, Rhode Island 02864

# Glossary

A.B.A. The American Badminton Association.

ACE. Winning point.

BACKHAND. Stroke hit on the left side of the body by right-handed players.

BACKSWING. That part of the swing which takes the racket back in preparation for the forward swing.

BASE. A spot on the middle line, slightly closer to the net than the baseline, to which, in singles, you should try to return after most shots.

BIRD. The missile used in badminton; same as shuttle or shuttlecock. See Chapter 13, pp. 84–85.

CLEAR. Stroke which lofts the bird to the back of the opponent's court.

CROSS-COURT. A stroke which sends the bird diagonally across the court.

DRIVE. A stroke that sends the bird in a relatively flat trajectory at a high rate of speed.

DROP SHOT. A stroke hit underhand or overhand from a point in the court away from the net which barely ·clears the tape and falls nearly vertically.

FAULT. Any one of various fouls which cost the server the serve.

FLICK. An especially quick movement of the wrist, accompanied by little arm motion, that sends the bird high and toward the rear of the opponent's court.

FLICK SERVE. A serve delivered with the motion described above.

FOLLOW-THROUGH. The smooth continuation of a stroke after the racket has met the bird.

FORECOURT. The front part of the court.

FOREHAND. Stroke hit on the right side of the body by right-handed players.

FRONT SERVICE LINE. Line parallel to, and 6½ feet from, the net on each side of the court, forming the forward boundary of the service courts.

GAME. Usually 15 points for men and 11 for women in singles, and 15 points in the various types of doubles. See Chapter 3, pp. 13–19, on basic rules and scoring about the "setting" of a game when, near the end, the score is tied.

HALF COURT. Court from which one player serves and, diagonally opposite, in which his opponent receives.

HIGH SERVE. A serve hit high and deep into the receiver's half court.

KILL. A hard, fast shot that cannot be returned.

LET. A term used to indicate that a point should, for reasons of unexpected interference that hinders play, be played over; also, the point itself that is to be played over.

LOB. Same as *Clear*.

LOB SERVE. Same as *High Serve*.

LOOSE SHOT. A weakly hit, vulnerable shot.

LOVE. In scoring, nothing or zero.

LOVE-ALL. Nothing to nothing; no score.

LOW SERVE. A softly hit serve that skims over the net.

MATCH. Best two out of three games.

MIXED DOUBLES. A four-handed game in which a man and a woman play as partners on each side.

NET SHOT. A form of drop shot or sharply struck shot played from a point near the net.

OVERHEAD. A stroke played from a point above head height.

PLACEMENT. A shot hit to a specific place in the opponent's court where it will be difficult to return.

POSITION. The point at which a player stands on the court at a particular time during a rally.

PUT-AWAY. Same as *Kill*.

RALLY. The exchanges across the net between sides before the end of a particular point.

RECEIVER. Player who receives the serve.

REPLY. Same as *Return*.

RETURN. The hitting back of an opponent's shot.

ROUND-THE-HEAD. An overhead smash stroke, using the forehand grip, played from the vicinity of the left shoulder.

SERVE. The act of putting the bird in play at the beginning of a rally.

SERVER. Player who delivers the serve.

SERVICE COURT. One of the two half courts into which the service must be directed.

SETUP. An easy chance to hit a winning shot.

SHORT SERVE. Same as *Low serve*.

SHORT SERVICE LINE. See *Front service line*.

SHUTTLE, SHUTTLECOCK. See *Bird*.

SMASH. A stroke hit downward with great speed and power.

STROKE. Act of hitting the bird with the racket.